*Dedicated to my parents,
Frederick and Gloria Haywood
for all they do and have done
for me and my daughters.
-Peaches*

Copyright © 2024 by Beatrice Whitley

All rights reserved. No part of this book may be reproduced or used in any manner without written permission of the copyright owner except for the use of quotations in a book review.

Book Design: Beatrice Whitley

Book Title: The Art of Staying Focused on Your Vision

ISBN 979-8-3031-1542-2 (paperback)

First paperback edition December 2024

Published by AWI Divine Publication/Beatrice Whitley
www.tricewhitley.me

TABLE OF CONTENT

CHAPTER TITLES	PAGE
INTRODUCTION	5
The Art of Staying Focused on Your Vision	7
The Power of Clarity of Purpose in Personal Life, Business, Ministry, and Relationships	10
Mastering Focus Through Boundaries in Personal Life, Business, Ministry, and Relationships	16
The Art of Staying Focused by Staying Connected to Your Source of Inspiration	22
The Art of Staying Focused by Celebrating Your Progress	28
The Art of Staying Focused by Having Patience	35

INTRODUCTION

Life can indeed be an extraordinary journey filled with a series of unpredictable twists and turns. At times, it can feel as though everything is aligning perfectly in your favor, like the universe is conspiring to support your every dream and endeavor. You might find yourself confidently stepping forward, embracing your ambitions, and feeling that sense of accomplishment that comes when the road ahead seems clear and your plans are materializing beautifully. But then, in an unexpected moment, it all seems to shift. The clear path you were once walking suddenly feels foggy, unsteady, and riddled with doubts and obstacles. You're left standing there, questioning every decision that once felt so certain. Have you ever been in such a place? It's a moment where mental and emotional exhaustion can feel heavy, almost paralyzing, and moving forward feels daunting.

In these challenging seasons, it's natural to feel unsure and ill-equipped. The confidence you once carried can vanish, and in its place may come feelings of inadequacy or fear. It's as though your mind has become unavailable, unwilling to engage with the very dreams you've nurtured for so long. You begin to wonder, "Was it all just an illusion? Did I truly make the right decisions? Was the vision that once felt so right even meant to be?"

These moments of questioning are not uncommon; in fact, they are part of the human experience. They are the crossroads where many feel tempted to give up or shrink back into the safety of the familiar. But the ultimate key to overcoming this phase is to stay focused on your vision. Even when doubt looms large and the noise of fear and uncertainty becomes deafening, anchoring yourself to your vision will provide you with the resilience you need. It is not about being blind to reality or ignoring the very real difficulties you may be facing. Rather, it's about tapping into the inner strength that comes from deeply understanding your purpose and the "why" behind your dreams.

Your vision is the guiding light in the storm. It's the promise you made to yourself when you first embarked on this journey. When you feel unsure, it's an invitation to revisit that vision, to remind yourself of the passion that ignited your path. What inspired you to start? What were the dreams that made your heartbeat faster? Allowing yourself to reconnect with that passion can reignite the fire within, even when you feel like the flame has dwindled.

In *The Art of Staying Focused on Your Vision,* you will discover the profound strength that comes from cultivating clarity, setting intentional boundaries, and staying deeply connected to your source of inspiration. This journey will reveal how to celebrate your progress and practice patience, creating a balanced life where personal, business, and ministry goals align harmoniously. You will learn strategies to navigate distractions with grace, embrace your growth with gratitude, and honor your commitments without losing sight of your core purpose. Ultimately, this book will equip you to transform your vision into reality, empowering you to live a life of focus, fulfillment, and unwavering determination.

TRICE WHITLEY

Do Right. Be Right. Live Right.

THE ART OF STAYING FOCUSED ON YOUR VISION

In a world filled with distractions, staying focused on your vision is one of the most powerful skills you can cultivate. It's not just about achieving your goals; it's about staying aligned with your purpose, no matter how chaotic or challenging life gets. Vision is the fuel that propels us forward, and the art of staying focused on it requires discipline, faith, and an unwavering commitment to the path ahead.

The first step in mastering this art is clarity of purpose. You need to understand why you are doing what you're doing. Your vision must be rooted deeply in your heart, because when life throws curveballs or the world tempts you with shiny distractions, it's your clarity of purpose that will keep you grounded. Knowing your "why" gives you the strength to say "no" to things that are misaligned with your true calling. It's what will keep you from veering off course when things get tough. When your purpose is clear, every decision becomes easier, because it's filtered through the lens of your vision.

Setting Boundaries is crucial in the art of focus. We live in a culture of constant noise—social media, societal pressures, and the endless stream of advice from people who may not fully understand your journey. It's easy to get caught up in trying to please others or to chase after every opportunity that comes your way. But real progress happens when you learn to say "no" to things that don't serve your vision. Boundaries help protect your time, energy, and focus. They create the space needed for you to keep working toward your goals without losing sight of them.

Another vital component is consistency. Staying focused isn't about making big, dramatic changes every once in a while. It's about showing up every single day and doing the work, even when you don't feel like it. Consistency builds momentum. Small, everyday actions are the building blocks of your vision. Even when the results aren't immediately apparent, trust that the seeds you're planting today will grow in time.

Staying Connected to Your Source of Inspiration is equally important. For those of faith, this means keeping God at the center of everything. In times of doubt or frustration, God is the ultimate source of strength and guidance. Staying connected to Him through prayer, meditation, or reading scripture helps realign your heart and mind with the vision He has for your life. When you face setbacks, it's important to remember that your vision is not only about you. It's part of something bigger. Leaning into your faith gives you the endurance and perspective you need to keep going.

It's also essential to celebrate progress, no matter how small. Staying focused on your vision can sometimes feel like a never-ending journey, but each milestone you achieve brings you closer to your ultimate goal. Take the time to acknowledge and celebrate your wins, even the little ones. This keeps you motivated and reminds you that you are making progress, even on the days that feel stagnant.

Finally, remember that patience is an art in itself. Great things take time, and the road to achieving your vision may not always be smooth. There will be setbacks, delays, and moments of doubt, but remember that nothing worth having happens overnight. Your vision will come to life, but it will unfold according to a divine plan, and your role is to trust the process. The key to staying focused is knowing that every step, every delay, and every struggle is part of the process.

The art of staying focused on your vision isn't about perfection or avoiding distractions altogether—it's about cultivating resilience, discipline, and trust. When you keep your eyes on your vision, maintain your boundaries, and stay connected to your source of inspiration, you'll find the strength to continue moving forward. Keep your purpose in front of you, and let nothing deter you from your God-given path. The world may throw distractions your way, but the one who is focused on their vision will always find a way to rise above them.

THE POWER OF CLARITY OF PURPOSE IN PERSONAL LIFE, BUSINESS, MINISTRY, AND RELATIONSHIPS

Staying focused on your vision requires a crystal-clear understanding of your purpose. Whether you're navigating your personal life, striving for business success, working in ministry, or building meaningful relationships, clarity of purpose is your compass, guiding every decision you make and every action you take. It's a powerful force that provides direction, strengthens resolve, and sustains motivation even through life's toughest challenges. Let's dive into how clarity of purpose impacts different areas of your life and how you can harness it to stay focused and steadfast.

Clarity of Purpose in Personal Life

Your personal life is the foundation upon which everything else is built. Having clarity about who you are, what you value, and what you aspire to achieve gives you a strong sense of identity. This clarity prevents you from being swayed by the opinions or expectations of others. It allows you to live authentically, making choices that align with your core values.

Start by asking yourself: What kind of life do I want to live? What are the things that truly matter to me? Maybe it's living a life of service, pursuing a passion, or building a family grounded in love and faith. Once you have a clear sense of your priorities, you can make deliberate decisions that move you closer to your ideal life. For instance, if health is important to you, you'll prioritize daily exercise and nutrition. If personal growth is your focus, you'll carve out time for learning and reflection.

In moments of temptation or distraction, returning to your purpose provides a powerful reminder of why you started in the first place. When the path gets difficult or progress seems slow, your purpose will motivate you to keep pushing forward. It's about understanding that every small action, even when it feels insignificant, contributes to the bigger picture. In this way, clarity of purpose in your personal life brings peace, focus, and fulfillment.

Clarity of Purpose in Business

In the world of business, clarity of purpose separates successful leaders from those who drift aimlessly. A clear purpose defines why your business exists beyond just making money. It informs your company's mission, vision, and values, shaping the culture and guiding strategic decisions. When you know the "why" behind your business, you can inspire your team, attract customers who share your values, and make choices that contribute to long-term growth rather than short-term gains.

Consider some of the most successful businesses. They are driven by a compelling purpose. For example, a sustainable clothing brand may have a mission to reduce the fashion industry's environmental impact. Every decision, from sourcing materials to marketing campaigns, aligns with this purpose. This kind of clarity not only drives focus but also builds trust with consumers and employees.

As a business leader or entrepreneur, ask yourself: What impact do I want my business to have on the world? How does it improve the lives of others? When challenges arise—because they inevitably will—having a clear purpose will anchor you, helping you navigate tough decisions. It will give you the courage to stay true to your values, even when it means sacrificing easier, more profitable paths.

Moreover, purpose-driven businesses often experience higher employee engagement. People want to work for organizations that stand for something. When your team understands and believes in the company's mission, they are more likely to stay focused, work collaboratively, and bring their best selves to the table. This shared sense of purpose fuels productivity and innovation, keeping the organization moving forward with unity and intention.

Clarity of Purpose in Ministry

In ministry, clarity of purpose is not just important—it's essential. Ministry work can be challenging, and without a clear understanding of your mission, it's easy to become overwhelmed or burned out. When you are serving others and spreading a message of faith, your purpose must be rooted in something greater than yourself. It must be anchored in your calling and the impact you want to make in the lives of others.

Ministry is all about serving God and His people. Ask yourself: Why did God call me to this work? What is the vision He has placed in my heart? Perhaps you feel called to uplift youth, spread the gospel to the unreached, or offer healing to the brokenhearted. Whatever it is, that purpose should drive every sermon you preach, every event you plan, and every interaction you have. It helps you maintain focus, even when the work feels thankless or the results aren't immediately visible.

When you have clarity of purpose in ministry, you can also guard against the temptation to compare yourself to others. It's easy to look at other ministries and feel inadequate, but your mission is unique. God's vision for you isn't meant to look like anyone else's. Staying focused on your calling allows you to use your gifts authentically and make the impact you were meant to make. Additionally, it empowers you to say "no" to opportunities that don't align with your purpose, freeing you to pour your energy into what truly matters.

Clarity of Purpose in Relationships

Relationships are a vital part of life, and having clarity of purpose here means knowing what you want and need in your connections with others. It's about understanding the values that are important to you in friendships, romantic partnerships, and even professional relationships. When you have this clarity, you can build connections that uplift, support, and inspire you, rather than drain your energy or distract you from your goals.

Think about your closest relationships. Are they aligned with your vision for your life? Do they encourage you to become the best version of yourself? Sometimes, we hold onto relationships out of fear or convenience, even when they are no longer serving us. Clarity of purpose allows you to evaluate your relationships honestly. It helps you identify those that are healthy and life-giving and those that may need to change or end.

This doesn't mean cutting people off without reason. It means being intentional about where and with whom you invest your energy. It also means knowing your non-negotiables in relationships. For example, if mutual respect and faith are critical values for you, you won't settle for anything less in a partnership. When you are clear about what you want, you can communicate openly and build stronger, more meaningful connections.

In romantic relationships, clarity of purpose helps you navigate challenges with a shared vision. It prevents you from getting sidetracked by petty conflicts and reminds you of the bigger picture. Whether you're building a family, supporting each other's dreams, or working together to serve your community, having a common purpose creates a foundation for lasting love and partnership.

The Ripple Effect of Clarity

Clarity of purpose in these areas—personal, business, ministry, and relationships—creates a ripple effect. When you know what you're working toward and why, you can align your daily actions with your long-term vision. You'll find that focus becomes less about discipline and more about devotion to what truly matters. Obstacles won't seem as daunting because you'll be anchored in a purpose that gives meaning to your struggles.

So, take the time to reflect, pray, and define your purpose in every area of your life. Write it down, revisit it often, and let it be your guide. Remember, clarity doesn't mean you'll never face doubt or distraction. It means you have the tools to refocus and realign when life tries to pull you off course. Stay committed, stay inspired, and never lose sight of the vision that was uniquely given to you.

MASTERING FOCUS THROUGH BOUNDARIES IN PERSONAL LIFE, BUSINESS, MINISTRY, AND RELATIONSHIPS

Staying focused on your vision, whether in personal growth, business pursuits, ministry endeavors, or relationships, requires more than just determination and drive. It demands the discipline to set and maintain strong boundaries that safeguard your purpose and well-being. These boundaries act as protective barriers, ensuring that distractions, burnout, and negativity don't derail your mission. Here, we explore how to establish boundaries to maintain focus in every area of your life.

Setting boundaries is a proactive act of self-respect and vision protection. It's about defining what is acceptable and what isn't, what you will allow into your life, and what you won't. When your boundaries are clear, you can more easily say "no" to distractions and "yes" to opportunities that align with your goals. By doing so, you conserve your energy, maintain mental clarity, and stay committed to your vision.

Boundaries are not barriers that isolate you from the world; rather, they are filters that help you prioritize what matters most. They provide the space needed to nurture your growth, work, ministry, and relationships. Let's break down how to set these boundaries in different areas of your life.

Setting Boundaries in Personal Life

Your personal life is your sanctuary, a place to recharge and reflect. Setting boundaries here means safeguarding your time, energy, and mental health.

1. Guard Your Time: Time is one of your most valuable resources. Schedule personal time for rest, hobbies, exercise, and spiritual practices, and treat these appointments as non-negotiable. Don't let other commitments infringe on this time. It's easy to feel guilty for prioritizing yourself, but remember: you can't pour from an empty cup. Taking time to rejuvenate keeps you energized and ready to pursue your vision.

2. Practice Digital Detox: In our hyperconnected world, constant notifications and social media can quickly erode your focus. Set boundaries with your devices. Designate "no-phone" times, such as during meals or an hour before bed. You might also consider having "offline" days where you disconnect entirely to reset your mind and reconnect with your purpose.

3. Know Your Priorities: Clarify what truly matters to you and make decisions that reflect these priorities. If spending time with loved ones or investing in personal growth is important, don't allow less significant activities to take precedence. Setting personal boundaries also means being selective about who you let into your inner circle. Surround yourself with people who uplift and encourage you, not those who drain your energy.

Setting Boundaries in Business

In business, the demands can be relentless, and without boundaries, work can easily consume every aspect of your life. To stay focused and avoid burnout, it's essential to establish clear professional boundaries.

1. Define Work Hours: If you're an entrepreneur or work from home, it's crucial to set strict work hours. Establish a start and end time for your workday and stick to it. This boundary helps you avoid overworking and ensures that you have time for personal and family life. Communicate these hours to your colleagues or clients, making it clear when you are and aren't available.

2. Manage Commitments Wisely: It's tempting to say "yes" to every opportunity, especially when trying to grow your business. However, spreading yourself too thin will only dilute your effectiveness. Evaluate every opportunity through the lens of your goals: Does it align with your vision? Will it contribute to your growth? If not, don't hesitate to decline politely. Remember, every "yes" you give means saying "no" to something else.

3. Create a Focused Workspace: Physical boundaries also play a role in maintaining focus. Designate a specific area for work that is free from distractions. Ensure that your workspace fosters productivity and clarity, whether that means having a clean desk, minimizing noise, or having everything you need within reach. If you work from home, communicate to family members when you are "in work mode" and shouldn't be disturbed.

4. Protect Your Mental Health: High-stress business environments can lead to burnout if you're not careful. Prioritize self-care and set boundaries that protect your mental health. This might mean taking breaks throughout the day, practicing mindfulness, or seeking professional support when needed. Don't feel guilty for stepping back when necessary; maintaining your well-being is essential for long-term success.

Setting Boundaries in Ministry

Ministry work often involves serving others, but it's crucial to balance this calling with self-care and intentional focus on your mission. Without boundaries, the demands of ministry can lead to exhaustion and a diluted sense of purpose.

1. Prioritize Your Calling: Ministry can be full of good opportunities that don't necessarily align with your primary calling. To stay focused, define your ministry's core mission and make it the foundation of every decision. It's okay to say "no" to events or initiatives that don't support this mission. God has given you a specific purpose, and honoring that calling requires discernment.

2. Set Emotional Boundaries: Ministry often involves helping people through difficult times, and it's easy to become emotionally drained. Practice setting emotional boundaries by recognizing when you need to step back and recharge. Seek support from mentors or counselors and don't hesitate to share the emotional load with trusted team members.

Remember, you are a vessel for God's work, but even vessels need time to refill.

3. Maintain a Sabbath Rest: God Himself rested on the seventh day, setting an example for us to follow. Schedule a weekly Sabbath where you rest from ministry work and focus on personal renewal. Use this time to pray, read scripture, spend time with loved ones, or simply enjoy God's creation. A Sabbath rest keeps you spiritually, mentally, and physically refreshed for the work ahead.

Setting Boundaries in Relationships

Relationships are a significant part of life, but without boundaries, they can become a source of distraction and tension. Setting boundaries in your relationships ensures that you nurture connections that support your vision and minimize relationships that pull you away from your purpose.

1. Communicate Your Needs: Open and honest communication is key to healthy boundaries. Share your goals and priorities with loved ones, and let them know how they can support you. If you need quiet time to work or space to focus on personal growth, communicate this lovingly but firmly. People who truly care about you will respect your boundaries.

2. Learn to Say No: It's not always easy to say "no," especially to people you care about. However, your time and energy are finite resources. If someone asks you to do something that conflicts with your priorities, practice saying "no" kindly but assertively. You can't be everything to everyone, and that's okay. Prioritizing yourself and your vision isn't selfish; it's necessary for achieving your purpose.

3. Evaluate Toxic Relationships: Not all relationships are beneficial. If someone consistently undermines your focus, disrespects your boundaries, or brings negativity into your life, it may be time to reevaluate that relationship. This doesn't mean you have to cut people off

completely, but you may need to distance yourself or limit interactions to protect your well-being and vision.

4. Foster Relationships That Uplift: Surround yourself with people who inspire you, challenge you to grow, and support your journey. These relationships will energize you and keep you focused on your purpose. Whether it's a mentor who provides guidance or a friend who offers encouragement, invest in connections that add value to your life and vision.

Mastering focus through setting boundaries is an art that requires intentionality and self-awareness. It's about creating a life where your personal well-being, business ambitions, ministry calling, and relationships align with your vision. Boundaries aren't about isolation but about curating a space where you can thrive, grow, and fulfill your purpose. By defining and upholding these boundaries, you protect your energy, stay true to your mission, and ultimately achieve the greatness you're destined for. Stay focused, stay inspired, and honor your vision by living with purpose and intentionality.

THE ART OF STAYING FOCUSED BY STAYING CONNECTED TO YOUR SOURCE OF INSPIRATION

In today's fast-paced and often chaotic world, staying focused on your goals and aspirations is more challenging than ever. The constant influx of distractions and responsibilities can easily derail even the most determined person. However, one of the most powerful ways to maintain focus is by staying deeply connected to your source of inspiration. Whether in personal, business, or ministry life, as well as in your relationships, this connection serves as a steady anchor that keeps you aligned with your purpose.

Your source of inspiration can vary depending on your beliefs, values, and aspirations. For some, it may be a deep spiritual connection with God or a higher power, while for others, it may be a vision of the future, the desire to make a positive impact, or the love and support of family and friends. Identifying and understanding what inspires you is crucial because it will be the fuel that keeps you moving forward, even when challenges arise.

Staying Connected in Your Personal Life

1. Cultivate a Daily Ritual: In your personal life, staying connected to your source of inspiration can be achieved through consistent daily rituals. For those, whose inspiration comes from their faith, this could mean spending time in prayer, meditation, or reading scripture. If your inspiration is rooted in personal growth or self-improvement, you might dedicate time each morning to journaling, visualizing your goals, or engaging in a gratitude practice. These rituals ground you and set the tone for the day, helping you stay focused and purposeful.

2. Create a Visual Reminder: Surround yourself with visual reminders of what inspires you. This could be a vision board, a meaningful quote on your desk, or a photo of your loved ones. When life gets overwhelming, these reminders will bring you back to your "why," reigniting your motivation and focus. Every time you see these symbols, you'll be reminded of what truly matters and why you're committed to staying on track.

3. Practice Mindful Presence: Being fully present in the moment can also keep you connected to your source of inspiration. Take time to savor life's simple pleasures—a walk in nature, a heartfelt conversation with a loved one, or a moment of silence to breathe deeply and feel grounded. Mindfulness strengthens your connection to your purpose, bringing clarity and calmness, which help you stay focused on your personal growth and dreams.

Staying Connected in Business Life

1. Align Your Work with Your Purpose: In the business world, it's easy to get caught up in the hustle and lose sight of why you started in the first place. Staying connected to your source of inspiration means consistently aligning your work with your core values and long-term vision. If your work is driven by a desire to help others, make sure that your business activities reflect that mission. If financial freedom for your family motivates you, remind yourself regularly of the life you're working to create.

2. Regularly Revisit Your Vision: Schedule time to reflect on your business goals and the original inspiration behind them. This could be done quarterly or even monthly. Ask yourself: "Am I still on track with my vision? Am I honoring the values that sparked my journey?" This reflection keeps you aligned with your purpose and prevents you from getting sidetracked by less meaningful tasks or opportunities.

3. Stay Inspired by Learning: Inspiration often wanes when we feel stagnant. Keep your passion for your business alive by continuously learning and growing. Read books written by leaders you admire, attend conferences, or join mastermind groups. Surrounding yourself with like-minded, driven people will reignite your enthusiasm and provide fresh perspectives that keep you focused.

4. Celebrate Small Wins: In the pursuit of big business goals, it's easy to overlook the progress you're making. Take time to celebrate small wins

and acknowledge your achievements. This not only boosts your confidence but also strengthens your connection to the source of your motivation. Recognizing your growth reminds you why you started and encourages you to keep moving forward.

Staying Connected in Ministry Life

1. Remain Rooted in Prayer and Reflection: Ministry work can be both fulfilling and draining. To stay focused, regularly reconnect with God or your spiritual source through prayer, meditation, or reflective practices. This connection provides guidance, strength, and a renewed sense of purpose, especially during difficult times. Starting each day with a moment of spiritual grounding can set the tone for the work ahead, reminding you that your ministry is a calling, not just a task.

2. Surround Yourself with a Faith Community: Ministry is not meant to be done alone. Stay inspired by engaging with a supportive community of fellow believers or ministry workers. These relationships can offer encouragement, accountability, and shared wisdom. When you're feeling discouraged or distracted, having people who uplift you and remind you of your mission can be invaluable.

3. Seek Out Testimonies and Stories: Hearing how your work has positively impacted others can be a profound source of inspiration. Whether through testimonies, letters of gratitude, or witnessing someone's transformation firsthand, these stories remind you that your ministry work has purpose and meaning. Let these moments refuel your passion and commitment to serving others.

4. Stay Focused on the Bigger Picture: In ministry, it's easy to get bogged down by day-to-day challenges or interpersonal conflicts. When this happens, take a step back and refocus on the bigger picture—spreading God's love, transforming lives, or building a faith-filled community. By staying connected to this greater purpose, you can navigate obstacles with grace and keep your eyes on the ultimate goal.

Staying Connected in Relationships

1. Prioritize Meaningful Connections: In relationships, your source of inspiration may be the love you have for your family, the joy of a close friendship, or the desire to support and uplift your partner. Stay connected to this inspiration by prioritizing quality time with those who matter most. Deep, meaningful conversations and shared experiences keep your relationships strong and fulfilling.

2. Practice Active Listening: One of the most powerful ways to stay connected in relationships is by truly listening. When you actively listen to your loved ones, you show that you value them and their presence in your life. This deepens the emotional connection and reminds you why these relationships are important to you. By staying present and engaged, you keep the relationship healthy and focused on mutual growth and understanding.

3. Maintain Healthy Boundaries: Relationships can be a source of both joy and distraction. To stay focused on your overall vision, set boundaries that protect your time and energy. Be clear about when you need space to work on your goals and when you're available to engage fully with loved ones. This balance ensures that your relationships support rather than hinder your progress.

4. Be Grateful and Give Back: Gratitude is a powerful connector. Regularly express appreciation to those who inspire and support you. Whether it's through a heartfelt thank-you note, an unexpected act of kindness, or simply telling someone how much they mean to you, gratitude keeps relationships strong and uplifting. Additionally, give back to those who inspire you, whether through mentorship, support, or simply being there when they need you.

    Staying focused on your vision requires a continuous connection to your source of inspiration. By cultivating daily rituals, aligning your work with your purpose, staying rooted in spiritual practices, and nurturing meaningful relationships, you create a life where focus flows naturally. Your inspiration becomes a guiding light, illuminating the path toward your dreams and giving you the strength to stay the course, no matter how difficult the journey may be.

In the end, remember that inspiration isn't a one-time event; it's something you must nurture and protect daily. By staying connected to what inspires you, you ensure that your focus remains unwavering, your purpose clear, and your heart full of passion and joy.

THE ART OF STAYING FOCUSED BY CELEBRATING YOUR PROGRESS

In our constant pursuit of goals and dreams, it's easy to become so future-oriented that we forget to pause and acknowledge how far we've come. Celebrating progress is an art that not only boosts our confidence but also reaffirms our purpose and keeps us focused on our journey. By taking the time to honor our achievements in personal, business, ministry, and relational spheres, we anchor ourselves in gratitude and build momentum for the future.

THE POWER OF CELEBRATION IN PERSONAL LIFE

1. Recognizing Personal Growth

Celebrating personal progress is an essential part of staying focused on self-improvement and self-awareness. Life is filled with challenges, and every victory, big or small, deserves acknowledgment. Maybe you've overcome a fear, developed a new habit, or made a decision that reflects your growth. Taking time to celebrate these wins reinforces the value of persistence and resilience.

Reflect on how you've evolved over time. For example, keeping a journal where you write down your accomplishments and breakthroughs can serve as a powerful reminder of your growth. On days when you feel stagnant or disheartened, looking back at these achievements can reignite your drive and renew your focus.

2. Establishing Reward Systems

Personal development can be a long and sometimes lonely road. By establishing reward systems for reaching milestones, you create a sense of excitement and anticipation. These rewards don't have to be extravagant; they can be something as simple as treating yourself to a day off, a new book, or a small getaway. Celebrating yourself helps you stay motivated and eager to continue on your path.

3. Practicing Gratitude for the Journey

Celebration in your personal life can also mean practicing gratitude for the progress you've made. Thank yourself for the dedication, effort, and courage you've shown. You can also express gratitude to those who've supported you. When you view your journey through the lens of gratitude, you stay grounded in appreciation, which helps you maintain clarity and focus on what truly matters.

THE IMPORTANCE OF CELEBRATION IN BUSINESS LIFE

1. Acknowledging Business Milestones

In the world of business, where the pressure to achieve results can be intense, it's crucial to celebrate milestones along the way. Whether it's completing a significant project, signing a new client, reaching a revenue goal, or launching a new product, each accomplishment is a testament to your hard work and strategic planning. Celebrating these wins energizes your team and reinforces the company culture you want to cultivate.

Create a tradition of celebrating wins within your business. Host small gatherings to honor achievements, give shout-outs during meetings, or send personalized messages of appreciation to team members. These gestures not only boost morale but also remind everyone of the progress being made, helping to sustain focus and motivation for future challenges.

2. Learning from the Process

Celebration in business is not only about the outcome but also about the process. Reflecting on what went well and what could be improved fosters a culture of continuous learning and adaptability. Celebrate the lessons learned and the resilience demonstrated in overcoming obstacles. By doing so, you create an environment where every experience, whether a success or a setback, contributes to growth and keeps you and your team aligned with the vision.

3. Keeping the Vision Alive

Celebrating business achievements keeps the vision alive and tangible. When you take time to acknowledge progress, you remind yourself and your team why you embarked on the journey in the first place. This sense of purpose is a powerful motivator. It keeps everyone focused on the overarching goals and the impact your business is striving to make in the world.

THE ROLE OF CELEBRATION IN MINISTRY LIFE

1. Honoring Spiritual Milestones

In ministry, the work is often about service, spiritual growth, and making a difference in people's lives. The journey can be both beautiful and challenging. Celebrating spiritual milestones, such as new members joining your ministry, a successful outreach program, or a breakthrough in someone's faith journey, reinforces the sense of purpose and divine calling.

These celebrations can be done through testimonies, special prayer services, or community gatherings where people share how the ministry has impacted their lives. Taking time to acknowledge these moments reminds you and your community of God's faithfulness and the impact of your service, helping you stay focused on your mission.

2. Reflecting on God's Work Through You

Sometimes, celebrating progress in ministry means reflecting on the work God has done through you. Recognize the small miracles and answered prayers along the way. Take moments to be still and express gratitude for the opportunity to be a vessel of God's love. When you pause to celebrate how God has moved in your ministry, you strengthen your faith and deepen your commitment.

3. Recharging for Future Service

Ministry can be demanding, and burnout is a real risk. Celebrating progress isn't just about honoring achievements; it's also about recharging for the work ahead. Hosting appreciation events for volunteers, taking time for spiritual retreats, or simply enjoying moments of fellowship keeps the spirit alive and the community strong. This rejuvenation helps everyone stay focused and inspired for future service.

CELEBRATING PROGRESS IN RELATIONSHIPS

1. Acknowledging Growth Together

Relationships are a significant part of our lives, and celebrating growth in this area is crucial. This could mean recognizing how communication has improved in a marriage, celebrating an anniversary, or acknowledging a friendship that has weathered storms. When you take time to celebrate relational wins, you strengthen the bonds and keep the relationship healthy and fulfilling.

Plan intentional celebrations, such as date nights, friendship getaways, or simple moments of acknowledgment. This not only keeps you focused on nurturing these connections but also creates beautiful memories that fuel the relationship's growth.

2. Expressing Appreciation

One of the most impactful ways to celebrate progress in relationships is by expressing appreciation. Let the people in your life know how much they mean to you and how grateful you are for their presence and support. Whether it's through a heartfelt letter, a thoughtful gift, or words of affirmation, celebrating the people you love keeps your relationships strong and focused on love and mutual respect.

3. Reflecting on How Far You've Come

Take time to reflect on the journey of your relationships. Maybe you've overcome misunderstandings, supported each other through difficult times, or achieved shared goals. Acknowledging these moments of progress keeps the relationship rooted in gratitude and purpose. It reminds you that the effort you put into nurturing these connections is worthwhile and meaningful.

WHY CELEBRATION FUELS FOCUS

1. Reaffirming Your "Why"

When you celebrate progress, you reaffirm your "why"—the reason you started in the first place. This sense of purpose keeps you focused and motivated. In personal life, it's a reminder of your commitment to growth. In business, it's a reminder of the impact you aim to make. In ministry, it's a reminder of your calling to serve. In relationships, it's a reminder of the love and support that sustain you.

2. Building Positive Momentum

Celebration builds positive momentum. Every time you acknowledge progress, you're creating a cycle of motivation and focus. It's easier to keep pushing forward when you feel a sense of accomplishment and joy. This momentum propels you through challenges and keeps you aligned with your vision.

3. Creating a Culture of Joy and Purpose

When you make celebration a habit, you create a culture of joy and purpose in every area of your life. It becomes a source of energy and strength, reminding you and those around you of the beauty of the journey. This culture keeps you focused, resilient, and inspired to keep striving for greatness.

The art of staying focused is greatly enhanced by celebrating progress. Whether in your personal life, business endeavors, ministry work, or relationships, taking time to acknowledge how far you've come fuels your passion and strengthens your commitment. Celebrate your journey, honor your growth, and let the joy of your progress propel you forward with renewed focus and unwavering purpose.

THE ART OF STAYING FOCUSED BY HAVING PATIENCE

Staying focused is an essential skill in achieving success and fulfillment in our personal, business, and ministry lives, as well as in maintaining healthy relationships. But often, what underpins the art of focus is an unglamorous yet transformative quality: patience. Patience provides the foundation for enduring through setbacks, waiting for the right opportunities, and allowing growth to happen in its natural course. In every area of our lives, cultivating patience is not just an exercise in delayed gratification but a testament to our commitment and faith in the journey.

PATIENCE IN PERSONAL LIFE

1. Understanding the Growth Process

Personal development is not a linear journey. It involves setbacks, moments of doubt, and periods of waiting. We live in a culture that celebrates speed—instant results, quick fixes, and fast success. However, true personal growth requires patience. Whether it's forming new habits, healing from past hurts, or learning a new skill, patience gives us the grace to accept where we are while we strive for where we want to be.

Staying focused in personal life involves setting goals and being persistent but also being patient enough to acknowledge that change takes time. For example, if you're working on developing a healthier lifestyle, patience allows you to celebrate small victories, like choosing a nutritious meal or making time for exercise, even if the physical changes take months to manifest. This patience keeps you grounded and prevents you from becoming discouraged.

2. Practicing Self-Compassion

Another aspect of patience in personal life is being compassionate with yourself. Too often, we beat ourselves up for not achieving milestones fast enough. The art of staying focused requires acknowledging that we are human, with strengths and limitations. Patience invites us to treat ourselves with the same kindness and understanding we would offer a friend. This self-compassion can rejuvenate our focus and give us the resilience needed to stay the course.

3. Trusting the Process

Patience also involves trusting the journey. When you set personal goals, whether it's improving your mental health or developing a new talent, the results won't come overnight. Trusting that every small effort contributes to a greater outcome helps you maintain your focus. Remind yourself that slow and steady progress is still progress, and patience becomes a source of strength, not frustration.

PATIENCE IN BUSINESS LIFE

1. Long-Term Vision Over Short-Term Gains

In business, having a long-term vision is crucial, and patience is what sustains that vision. It's tempting to chase quick profits or make hasty decisions to keep up with competition. However, staying focused on your overarching goals requires the discipline to think beyond immediate gratification. Patience ensures that you're investing in sustainable growth, whether that means building a brand, nurturing customer relationships, or developing a quality product.

For entrepreneurs, patience can mean enduring the early struggles of a startup without giving up. It might take months or even years to see the fruits of your labor, but having the patience to weather the storms can lead to greater rewards in the future. By staying focused on your mission, you create a foundation that's more resilient to setbacks.

2. Navigating Setbacks Gracefully

Business life is filled with unexpected challenges. Deals fall through, strategies don't always work, and competitors might gain an edge. The art of staying focused in these moments is made possible through patience. Instead of reacting impulsively, patience gives you the ability to assess the situation calmly and make thoughtful decisions.

Moreover, patience fosters a growth mindset. When a project doesn't yield the expected results, a patient approach allows you to analyze what went wrong, learn from the experience, and apply those lessons moving forward. This level of focus keeps you adaptive and forward-thinking, even when things don't go as planned.

In business, relationships are everything. Building trust with colleagues, clients, and partners takes time. Patience in networking and relationship-building ensures that connections are genuine and mutually beneficial. It's easy to get frustrated when you don't see immediate results from your efforts to expand your network or secure a partnership, but patience reminds you that some of the most meaningful opportunities come from seeds planted long ago. Staying focused means nurturing these relationships consistently and authentically, knowing that the payoff may not be immediate.

PATIENCE IN MINISTRY LIFE

1. Waiting for God's Timing

Ministry work is deeply spiritual and often requires waiting for God's timing. It's easy to become impatient when the impact of your work isn't immediately visible, or when prayers seem unanswered. However, the art of staying focused in ministry is rooted in faith and patience. Trusting that

God has a plan, even when you can't see it, gives you the strength to continue serving with a joyful heart.

Patience in ministry also means being present for people's spiritual journeys, which often take time. Whether you're mentoring someone in their faith or leading a congregation, it's crucial to recognize that transformation is gradual. Staying focused on your calling means being patient and trusting that your efforts, guided by God, are making a difference.

2. Enduring Challenges with Grace

Ministry work can be challenging, from facing criticism to dealing with burnout. Patience allows you to endure these hardships with grace, keeping your focus on God's purpose for your life. It reminds you to seek guidance in prayer and trust that the trials you're facing have a purpose. This spiritual patience keeps your heart centered and your mind steadfast.

3. Celebrating Small Wins

In ministry, it's important to celebrate small victories, such as a successful event, a meaningful sermon, or someone expressing gratitude for your work. Patience helps you see the value in these moments, even if the larger goals are still a work in progress. By focusing on the positive impact you're having, you stay motivated and aligned with your purpose.

PATIENCE IN RELATIONSHIPS

1. Understanding Growth in Relationships

Relationships, whether romantic, familial, or friendships, are built over time. They require nurturing, communication, and understanding. Patience is crucial for maintaining focus on the health and growth of these connections. People change, and challenges arise, but the art of staying focused means being committed to working through difficulties rather than seeking immediate resolutions.

Patience allows you to give your loved ones the space they need to grow and evolve. It also gives you the grace to forgive and understand, rather than reacting impulsively. This creates a foundation of trust and respect, which is essential for any strong relationship.

2. Practicing Active Listening

One way to show patience in relationships is through active listening. When conflicts arise or when someone you care about needs to share something important, patience enables you to listen without interrupting or immediately offering solutions. Staying focused on understanding their perspective strengthens the bond and shows that you value the relationship.

3. Giving Relationships Time to Mature

Some relationships take longer to blossom than others. Whether it's a friendship that develops slowly or a romantic relationship that requires time to build a solid foundation, patience is key. Staying focused means not rushing the natural course of these connections. It's about valuing quality over speed and recognizing that true, lasting bonds are formed through consistent care and understanding.

THE BENEFITS OF CULTIVATING PATIENCE

1. Reduced Stress and Anxiety

Patience naturally reduces stress. When you're not constantly worried about achieving everything immediately, you're able to approach life with a sense of calm. This helps you stay focused and present in the moment, which is essential for effective decision-making and maintaining emotional well-being.

2. Greater Resilience

Patience builds resilience. It helps you accept that setbacks are part of the journey and gives you the strength to bounce back. This resilience keeps you focused on your long-term goals and prevents you from giving up prematurely.

3. Enhanced Focus and Clarity

When you're patient, you're not easily distracted by the urgency to have it all figured out. Instead, you're able to focus on the task at hand, knowing that each step you take is leading you closer to your goals. Patience provides clarity and prevents you from being overwhelmed by the pressures of instant results.

The art of staying focused is deeply intertwined with the practice of patience. Whether in personal development, business ventures, ministry work, or relationships, patience allows us to move through life with grace, resilience, and unwavering focus. It reminds us that true success is often a slow build, a series of small, consistent actions that accumulate over time. By embracing patience, we honor the journey and keep our eyes on the greater vision, confident that our efforts will bear fruit in due season.

Mastering the art of staying focused while maintaining a balanced lifestyle requires an intentional blend of clarity, boundaries, inspiration, patience, and the celebration of progress. It begins with understanding your purpose and using that clarity to filter out distractions, ensuring every choice aligns with your values and goals. In both personal and professional life, setting healthy boundaries is essential to protect your time and energy, allowing you to dedicate your efforts to what truly matters. Staying connected to sources of inspiration—be it through spiritual practices, meaningful relationships, or personal passions—fuels your motivation and keeps your vision alive. Celebrating progress, no matter how small, fosters a sense of accomplishment and reinforces the importance of the journey, not just the destination. Embracing patience helps you navigate setbacks and trust in the process, recognizing that growth often takes time and perseverance. By integrating these elements, you create a harmonious and fulfilling life where focus is not a fleeting effort but a sustainable way of living. This approach empowers you to pursue your goals with resilience, while also finding joy, peace, and purpose in the present moment.

Empowerment comes from understanding that feeling unequipped doesn't mean you are. Sometimes, setbacks and doubts are opportunities in disguise, allowing you to grow in ways you never anticipated. You may have to learn new skills, adapt your plans, or even rest and recharge before moving forward. These experiences build resilience and character. Instead of fearing the shift, embrace it as a chance to evolve, to become even more prepared for the challenges and victories ahead.

Inspiration lies in the realization that every great dreamer has faced moments of uncertainty. It's a shared human experience, and many who have achieved greatness did so by pushing through these very moments. You, too, can move past this. Hold fast to your vision, and remind yourself that setbacks are not a signal to stop but a call to persevere. Stay inspired by knowing that growth often happens in discomfort, and your journey, with all its unpredictability, is leading you toward something beautiful. You are equipped, even if you don't feel like it now, and the path forward will become clearer one brave step at a time.

DATE   /   /

DATE   /   /

www.ingramcontent.com/pod-product-compliance
Lightning Source LLC
Chambersburg PA
CBHW030115230526
45469CB00005B/1647